T0157514

COCOON TO BUTTERFLY

Devotional Journal

Be True

Be You

Be Free

Toshia Griffin

authorHOUSE

AuthorHouse™
1663 Liberty Drive
Bloomington, IN 47403
www.authorhouse.com
Phone: 833-262-8899

Published by AuthorHouse 04/24/2023

ISBN: 979-8-8230-0256-1 (sc)
ISBN: 979-8-8230-0271-4 (e)

Print information available on the last page.

Any people depicted in stock imagery provided by Getty Images are models, and such images are being used for illustrative purposes only.
Certain stock imagery © Getty Images.

Contact Information:
C2Coutreach15@gmail.com
Subject line BOOKS

Editor: Candice Shields
WYS Solutions Consulting
contact@wyssolutions.com

All scriptures quoted or copied from the New King James (NKJ) Edition and New International Version (NIV) Bibles

This book is printed on acid-free paper.

Dedication

To Don' Sha, Tro'Sha, and Tia', my angels, my inspiration, and my motivation; 3 of my reasons for living. My heart is filled with joy each day God allows me to wake up as your mother. Thank you all for all you do to keep me going. Daughters, Friends, Prayer partners!!

I love you Always!! Mommy

To my grand children Dre', Jay, and Lei'Lei Thank you for always helping me and saying, "you can do it, Granny". I love you all soooo much !!!

To Pastor Bridget Jones, my cousin and friend; I love you. Thank you for taking out the time to discuss the hard things with me and listening to me as well (sometimes :). You have been a major reckoning force in my time of come back. I Love You BFFC

Apostle Julie Hitchens, thank you for continuously being a light and pushing force in my life. (2004-present) Always speaking into my life with truth and wisdom. Mother Apostle, I love you.

Apostle Donnell and Pastor Stephanie Vigers, you are rare jewels in the body of Christ. Loving, Patient, & Compassionate; Mentors to be cherished. Thank You for all the encouragement, wisdom, and pushing. You've led and taught by example; supported and participated in ministry; all while speaking into my life. I love and appreciate you both very much !!! 2013- present

Introduction

God, I wonder where I would be, if you hadn't covered me and watched over me all my life. The night clubs, the weird motel rooms with strange folks, the wild parties, the adults that took advantage of me, the old men that bought me and the women that used me. God, it was only You that I didn't end up dead, strung out, or ill from some incurable disease. I was thousands of miles away from home and you brought me back alive, in one piece and in my right mind. I could never thank you enough God!!! All the praises and glory go to you!!!! People look at me and think they have me all figured out. But God, You and you alone made me (created me) to be separate and to stand alone in your glory!!! My blindness was to the glorifying of God!   *John 9:3,6-8*

This devotional is to edify, encourage, and exhort the body of Christ!! To edify the believers, to encourage the broken-hearted and discouraged, to extend an invitation of fellowship to the non- believers and back sliders, and to exhort the Name of Jesus!! From Cocoon to Butterfly Daily Devotional is a book created in love and hope to reach other women and men that may feel they have no way out of their hidden hurts and situations, while for others hoping and praying for a loved one, daughter or son to return home from their long prodigal journey. I pray that somewhere in these pages of scripture and testimonies your hope is renewed, your heart is lifted, and you get a fresh wind and keep praying for that soul that's dear to you and God!

I'm a Butterfly

April 11, 2014, at 5:02pm

God gave me the revelation about the Butterfly and Our lives! The greatness in us is being birthed right now.

From the dust and grime of life, we retreat to our cocoons (caves) for restoration, rebuilding, and rejuvenation. We spend the allotted time in this state, awaiting the time that God will call us forth into our new-found greatness.

The ugliness of the cocoon {surrounded by our own dirt, loneliness, rejection, and despair} the weirdness of being a caterpillar {different, too much baggage, filthy mind sets, so many things and distractions {we feel like we have 6 legs} No one cares for us, likes us, and sometimes no one even loves us in our lowest states of life.

We don't like ourselves in some instances. In our worse state God, himself sees us. He chooses us, uses us, redeems us, and Jesus intercedes for us!!! He makes us into this wonderful creation. {Old things are passed away and all things become new}

2 Corinthians 5:17 King James Version (KJV) 17: Therefore, if any man be in Christ, he is a new creature: old things are passed away; behold, all things become new.

SOME PEOPLE STILL CAN'T OR WON'T ACCEPT THE BEAUTY OF WHAT WE'VE BECOME. IT'S OKAY, BECAUSE THERE'S A WHOLE WORLD OUT THERE THAT ADMIRES OUR GOD GIVEN BEAUTY!!!

I'M A BUTTERFLY

SHEDDING MY COCOON...

GOD BLESS YOU!!!!

TABLE OF CONTENTS

Note: Any time during these lessons, if you feel depressed or extremely sad and/or recognize any triggers to addictions, Please STOP the lessons and contact your pastor, mentor, sponsor, prayer partner, or loved one that you trust to pray with you and give you sound doctrine that can help you medically and physically. Resume your self-help only after you've dealt with the emotions that arose doing these lessons.

Supplies needed: pen or pencil, notebook, or journal.

Open your heart and ears & have a desire to be better!!

Unit I Part 1
Walking out the Process

Father God in the name of Jesus Christ, we pray that every spirit of rejection be broken, and your people be set free. God, we call forth wholeness and healing to every hurting heart. Touch every reader and intercessor right now who will turn these pages. Jesus will redeem us from whatever hurts, rejections, discouragements, setbacks, let downs, disappointments, deception, abandonment, and any hidden agendas of friends and family. We pray right now God, and we allow you into our hearts and minds to remove the band aids and truly heal us. God, I call forth truth and comfort of the Holy Spirit, our comforter and the delivering blood of Jesus to cover our emotions and minds and bring us to a place of wholeness and deliverance forever. I command that every demonic activity in our minds and lives cease now, in Jesus name. Amen.

Rejection

I personally know rejection all too well. I felt that if I share some of my testimonies with you, it may help you to see your way through a hard spot in your life. I think if I talk about rejection from within the family setting it may set the tone for you to open up and relate to other areas of hurt which may have stemmed from some of your early family issues. We like to call it the under-currents. See, the undercurrents keep surfacing all throughout our lives. They don't die until they are truly exposed and dealt with from the root to the surface. We go years and years with these hurts and rejections haunting us and all that we do is affected by them. Sometimes we don't know until we've sabotaged ourselves in so many ways. {Psalms 27:9-10}

I'll tell you a story about a little girl in a second-class neighborhood, with a hard-working mother and a loving, sweet grandmother. She wore expensive clothes; her mom had a decent job back in the 70's. Her grandmother took exceptionally loving care of her; dressed her beautifully, and even made some of her clothes by hand. But this little girl was missing something especially important. She did not feel loved by her mom who she loved very much. She believed her mother loved her, but there was some type of spiritual barrier fighting against their relationship from the very beginning. She loved her grandmother dearly, but she always fought for her mother's attention. She seemed to always get only some of it and never enough to make her feel content. So, the spirit of rejection set in at a really early age. One day the young girl sat on the curb and said out of her mouth, "My momma does not like me". Don't you know that day the enemy took her statement and ran with it. He magnified the situation to a point where the girl and her mother really ended up not liking each other. By the time she was a teenager, the two really had a true dislike for one another for many reasons that ensued.

Over the years their communication continuously went downhill, and their relationship was horrible. The young girl was so close to her grandmother that she almost disregarded her mother all together. The mother was so disappointed in her daughter's actions throughout her teenage years, that she almost didn't want to look at the girl. As a matter of fact, she sent the girl away to live with her dad by the age of twelve. Not, to mention the mother remarried and had another baby by the time the first daughter was ten years old. This only added another layer to the feeling of rejection. The first daughter had already felt ignored by the mother, and now she had a new baby that she must see after, and she really couldn't spend time with the older child. The mother had a husband and a full-time job, plus she started a home-based business. Her life and plate were full; by the time this girl reached the age of fifteen, she felt like she wasn't wanted or loved by her mom and at the age of sixteen, she decided that she was going to leave home and live on her own. She doesn't need her mother or stepdad anymore.

Do you see the under-currents? Rejection, abandonment, and loneliness. The child goes out into the world seeking love, wanting a void filled in her life that only her mother could give her. She goes into the world immature and thirsty for attention; that only her mom could satisfy. She starts her prodigal child journey.

This young girl was raised in the church, saved, and received Christ at an early age, spoke in tongues and experienced dreams and visions from God. You see, the trip to dad's house at twelve years old, introduced her to a true encounter with Jesus. She felt like the only person who understood her was her grandmother, who always kept an open and honest communication with her. She leaves home with a young guy five years older than herself and starts an adult relationship. While trying to play wife to this man and go to school, she finds it's all too much for her. He cheats on her and leaves her for another girl. Here it is again, rejection and abandonment. This young woman gets introduced to exotic dancing by an older friend and meets another man who introduces her to teenage prostitution and illicit sex scandals. She survives that and comes back home as a bisexual female. Later she got with another man whom she married and had daughters with. Throughout this relationship she was physically and mentally abused. During all of that, she was seduced by an older female who also played mind games and manipulated her. The older woman also rejected her and left her out in the world for the wolves. (That story is the book "Lost in the House")

The attention of the older women and men took the place of the love and attention that she didn't receive from her mother and father. The older people in her life taught her, loved her, and gave her lots of attention, spoiled her, gave her money, told her how pretty she was and made her feel wanted and loved; all while controlling her and misusing her body. Do you see the downward spiral? She ended up not respecting men, loving women, disrespecting herself in every way possible, and never understanding that this all stemmed from that troubled relationship between her and her mother. It wasn't until she recovered from prostitution, stripping, lesbianism, an abusive marriage and multiple dysfunctional bad relationships with women and the death of her dear grandmother, that she realized, she was in a destructive mind state and had no idea how to get out of it. She started to search for answers with counselors and therapist in various places. She felt like she was losing her grip and nothing or nobody could help her. She even tried suicide, but God himself would not let her off the hook. She heard the Lord say, "you will not pass out or fall asleep. You will stay awake and watch everything that is happening; because you will never try this again."

This lady thought to herself, "There's got to be a way out of this hole I've dug for myself". From that day forth she searched medically, mentally, and spiritually for some kind of relief and help for her pain. She rededicated her life to the Lord and found a good bible-based church for her and her 3 daughters.

They started going to church. After joining a few churches and seeking God for herself, studying the word of God to show herself approved and praying and believing the promises of God. While it was not an immediate change, eventually things started to get better for this lady. Her children were blessed and favored. Every school they went to, they excelled, and they were always recognized for their achievements. She was so proud of her children and her children called her blessed. Over time, they became an unstoppable team of determined young women and God kept fighting for them.

The hurt she experienced from and with her mother and her father was the reason she showed her own daughters extreme love, attention, and compassion. She didn't want to ever be apart from her daughters; and she had to learn as they grew older that she had to let them go to live their lives. Again, as an adult learning to put aside abandonment and rejection; her children had to go and live adult lives and learn things for themselves, just as she did. She felt her children were the only people in the world who she would never lose, and they would always be together. She was extremely attached and overly protective of her daughters which made it extremely difficult for them to move away and live their own lives when time came to do so. She had never lived alone, here she was forty-three years old and experiencing new growing pains of her kids being grown and leaving her house. She was stuck experiencing anxiety, PTSD, and depression because she had not conquered the under-currents (the demons) in her life. All of it came to her front and center, it all made a full circle. The realization of the undercurrents came up all at once, that she pressed through her whole life and had not taken the time to really heal from any of it. She relived all the hurts, pains, disappointments, rejections, rape, disgusting moments, humiliating scenes, degrading situations, the failed relationships, and even belittling arguments with her ex-husband, right down to the night she was drunk and tried to commit suicide. She was forced to deal with them all at once.

It was time to grow up or die.

I want you to think of some undercurrents that you have. You must be completely honest with yourself. Think long and hard about what you wanted from your parents that you didn't get, and how that may have caused you to be or not to be a certain way as an adult. Now, write them down and look at how those same undercurrents caused you to make certain decisions that weren't as positive as you would have liked for them to be.

While thinking about those things, also think about how you have grown or need to grow in those areas now as an adult. I'm going to give you a few scriptures to focus on while you are doing this and make sure you pray, sincerely. Open your heart, mind, and spirit for God to come in and make the necessary changes. Open your ears, so that you can hear him clearly when he speaks, because he will speak, if you let him. Dig deep for your undercurrents. They may be jealousy, rejection, abandonment, low self-esteem, etc.; let's describe the ugliness of the first cocoon.

My Thoughts and Emotions

_____

_____

_____

_____

Sometimes, the rejection is deeply rooted in us, we just can't see our way out. Causing us to be "Lost in the House" let's think about the deception and rejection we feel in school, work, and relationships all the time. We didn't get picked for the cheerleader team, or the football team, the popular kids didn't want to have anything to do with you. You're an adult and you work really hard to be recognized on your job, but they give the promotion to the new guy that you trained. Oh man, "what's wrong with this picture", you ask? "I taught them everything they know", you think to yourself.

Here comes anger and rejection, "what's wrong with me" "why didn't I get picked"? The man or woman of your dreams marries another woman and leaves you sitting at home watching movies alone. You loved him or her with all your heart and he or she cheats on you and makes you feel like you aren't good enough to be with them. We all know these feelings all too well. {Matthew 18:27, 35; Nahum 1:7}

The first abandonment, rejection, and self-esteem issues we experience are at home and/or in school, or in church. The time has come to think of sometimes that you felt angry because you were rejected.

My Thoughts and Emotions

_____

_____

_____

_____

_____

The questions in the following sections are designed to have you look back into your life and find the beginning of the undercurrents. Identify them, approach them in the spirit, and pray. Answer them truthfully; no matter how painful it may become. If you want to be whole and healed, you must be honest with yourself. As we work through these areas together, you will find it a little difficult to face some truths about yourself at first. Keep reading and writing- it will become easier as we move from unit to unit.

While reflecting, I also want you to try and identify who God called you to be! I want you to think about that small still voice that you heard as a child, or a teen, or even as an adult telling you what He (God) wanted from you, or something He wanted you to do. You weren't imagining things; at the time you may not have understood that it was Him speaking.

What's one thing that God has spoken to your heart about you? (Example: I heard at a young age I would be used by God to do great things)

_____

_____

_____

_____

_____

1. Who was the first person that broke your heart? (parents, family, lovers)

_____

_____

_____

_____

2. When did they break your heart? (childhood, teenager, young adult)

_____

_____

_____

_____

3. How do you feel about them now? (presently)

_____

_____

_____

_____

4. How did you feel about them then? (hate, sad, hurt, angry)

_____

_____

_____

_____

I'm a Butterfly!!

5. How did that heartbreak affect how you feel about certain people and areas of your life? (men/ women, mother figures, father figures etc.)

_____

_____

_____

_____

Depending on how many incidents you named in the beginning of the exercise, I want you to name 2 more incidents in the last 10-12 years when your heart has been broken.

_____

_____

_____

_____

<u>Unit 1 Part 2</u>
<u>Walking out your Process</u>

In Jesus name, we call out every spirit that is not like God!! We call out every spirit of deception, anger, rage, disappointment, and discouragement; now in Jesus name. God, you know us all name by name, and face by face; we ask that you go back into our minds and hearts and deliver us from the anger buried deep in our souls and hidden places. We command the enemy to take his hands off our minds and hearts, and we decree and declare we are free today. We choose to forgive the abusers, users, manipulators', deceivers, and rejecters that have been in our lives!! We choose to drop it off today and carry it with us no further! In Jesus name Amen!!!

<u>Anger</u>

Some of us have suffered and still suffer with rage, an irate temper and/or bad attitudes. If we would truly allow God to come into our hearts and help us to walk into His perfect plan for our lives, then and only then can we truly be healed and delivered.

This young girl grew into a strong, independent angry young woman - always ready to defend herself by any means necessary. She felt the need to prove her point to anyone who made her feel less than or inadequate. Honestly, she didn't need to prove anything to anyone. However, her previous rejection and discouragement caused her to feel like she was not good enough and always had to prove that she was right.

Instead of standing in confidence, she felt defeated. In actuality, she knew she was pretty, smart, funny, and outgoing, but she didn't feel victorious, free, delivered, nor prosperous.

She knew she was free because Jesus died on the cross for her freedom. She knew she was victorious and delivered, because she was fearfully and wonderfully made in the image of God and the blood of Jesus Christ was shed for her deliverance. We often know a lot of things that we don't apply to our lives. Someone may know that they have a wonderful voice; but never uses it to their advantage and end up living a life of poverty instead of applying their gift and using their voice to make a living. They know they have the talented gift of song, but never apply themselves; it, therefore serves them no purpose. That's a small example of what I'm about to reveal to you.

To be clear, I knew in my mind that I was wonderfully made, but I didn't feel it in my heart. I, therefore, did not live like I was wonderfully made. I didn't apply the love of God to every area of my life, which caused me to walk around in constant self-doubt and bound by shame from my past mistakes. I was angry, because no one understood me; when newsflash, I did not even understand myself. How could anyone else understand this whirl wind mind frame I was in most of the time. There was no peace, self-control, or temperament operating in my life. Anger, rage, stress, frustration, irritation, and loneliness was always present; drowning out God's peace that surpasses all understanding, even our own. Pushing back caused God's unfailing love that covers a multitude of sin; His unspeakable joy, which flushes out all anxiety, frustration, and stress, to be out of sight to me.

Why? I'm glad you asked. I was so angry at my mom and dad for playing favoritism to my siblings and turning their backs on me. I was angry and enraged with my ex-husband because I felt like he did not show me the same love that I gave him for so many years. The abuse and mistreatment that I suffered was just unnecessary and stupid. The rage that stemmed from the shame of teenage prostitution and exotic dancing, always made me feel like people were looking down on me and judging my every move. I was bullied in elementary school, and by the time I got to junior high school I was fighting everybody. I fought my battles and other kids battles too. I could not stand to see anyone be picked on; the act would push me to jump in on their behalf.

The bible says, "be angry and sin not," well, I will be honest, I would always sin when I got angry. I made up curse words, I had my own vocabulary of words to say to people. I also, held grudges, walking in unforgiveness. One big problem is I was an only child, and I had what is called the "only child mentality". We all know that it is said that those who are only children are spoiled. I have seven siblings; one half-sister from my mom and six other siblings by my father; but I'm the only child for my mom and dad; but they both favored my other siblings, and my birth right was thrown to the side like it was nothing. I am my mother's oldest child, and the second oldest of my dad's children. I am sure you see at this point the rising of rejection and anger was becoming my under- current. Sensitivity from emotional bruises made it exceedingly difficult for anyone to truly get close to me.

The experiences of rejection repeatedly, really took a toll on my self-esteem. These feelings began with my parents, and progressed when I was introduced to exotic dancing. Add the experience with my first true love, who left me at our apartment and married another woman after we had a bad argument. He came back seven days later and said, "I need this apartment; you cannot afford it anyway", and commenced to moving me out and dropped me off at my mother's house. He and his new wife moved in the next day. As if those incidents were not enough, I was included into a prostitution ring, and was turned out by an older married woman who manipulated and controlled me for five years. I then married a man who I thought I would be with forever, and gave birth to his children, only for him to become emotionally, verbally, and physically abusive.

Without fail, I had become the worse version of myself.

I was angry, hurt, disappointed, ashamed, rejected, and felt like the lowest. God would not let suicide steal His purpose from me. These negative characteristics ruled my life and actions for years. I was walking in my calling, and those under-currents still hindered me from reaching my full potential. It was not until I truly saw myself as God saw me, allowed Him to renew my mind, opened my heart to myself the way I did towards others. I started to love myself and put me first. I loved Toshia. I wanted to make beautiful meals for me, I wanted to cuddle the little hurt girl and tell her that she was enough, that she mattered, and I loved her very much. I forgave her for making so many dumb mistakes. I reminded her of God's unchanging love for her. I told her that she could stop fighting her own battles and being angry. Because, God, Jesus, and our assigned angels are standing by waiting for us to let Him take care of us and fight our battles with those who should have loved us.

I'm here to tell you that anger and rage will not go away until you truly choose to let it go. You choose to stay angry. Let them folks off the hook and go on with your Father who is preparing a table before all your enemies. Love your hurt self, your abused self, your deceived, mistreated, raped, promiscuous, cheated, disliked, addicted self. Love that part of yourself and forgive that part. I don't care how far back you must go; go find the little you and help her or him heal. Talk to the little you and revive, restore, and rest the little hurt one. Once you do that, bring that part of you up to speed and allow the grown-up you to make mistakes, but do not stay in those feelings too long. Get up quickly and monitor every thought while in this process, just as the bible tells us to pull down every thought that tries to exalt itself over the things of God.

Believe God every step of the way. Anger and disappointment bring body pains. Unforgiveness can birth cancer, diabetes, and Alzheimer's.

There is evidence to show that suppressed anger can be a precursor to the development of cancer, and a factor in its progression after diagnosis. Thomas, S P et al. "Anger and cancer: an analysis of the linkages." Cancer nursing vol. 23,5 (2000): 344-9. doi:10.1097/00002820-200010000-00003

{Stress is critically involved in the development and progression of disease. From the stress of undergoing treatments to facing your own mortality, the physiological processes that stress drives have a serious detrimental effect on the ability to heal, cope and maintain a positive quality of life. This is becoming

*increasingly clear in the case of neurodegenerative diseases.}
Justice NJ. The relationship between stress and Alzheimer's
disease. Neurobiol Stress. 2018 Apr 21;8:127-133. doi: 10.1016/j.
ynstr.2018.04.002. PMID: 29888308; PMCID: PMC5991350.*

*"Every stress leaves an indelible scar, and the organism pays
for its survival after a stressful situation by becoming a little
older" <u>Hans Selye (1950)</u>*

Jesus wants us to respond as he did. Father, forgive them for
they know not what they do. He says this because when people do
us wrong, they do not know what they are doing to themselves by
messing with God's child. They do not realize the consequences
they'll suffer as a result of mistreating God's kids. WE ARE
CHILDREN OF THE KING!!! Smile, pray for the ones that hurt
you (not asking God to get em'), and watch our Father fight for us.
In Jesus Name. Amen.

Now, you know when we respond to things while we're
angry, most times we do the wrong thing. If we open our mouths
with rage in our hearts, we certainly will say the wrong things.
Anger and rage have cost so many lives to be lost unnecessarily,
relationships to be broken prematurely, and marriages have
ended; all because, we as people don't want to 'shut up' and listen
to the other person. We tend to press our issue and make it more
about how we feel, and we do not even think about how it made
the other person feel. Most times women tend to fall for the victim
role. We often push our mates away with all that (I, I, I, me, me,
me), stuff. Do you know what actions you take that other in your
life, specifically your significant other may not like or care for? Do
you even care that you do and say things that may hurt, offend, or
upset someone else? Pride is a BIG spirit that comes sometimes
from rejection. We think more of ourselves than we should. The
bible speaks against a prideful spirit, and calls those of us who are
easily angered, fools. (**Psalm 34:14**) "Be not quick in your spirit
to become angry, for anger lodges in the heart of fools."

Self -Control is a fruit of the spirit, along with temperance,
and patience. Whether you have the Holy Ghost or not; you
know what these words mean. If you're not operating in them,

you're not walking in the love of God. We must take this Love Walk profoundly serious. It's the bridge between us and our final destination; Heaven or Hell.

Your love walk can also be the deal breaker to the proper introduction of Jesus to others, through our lives, if it is not where or what God says it should be. We can cause others to stumble or turn them away from God. Do we really look, act, or sound like Jesus? When we're angry, do we still exemplify the characteristics of our savior, Jesus? I have a friend that is so very sensitive, she thought one day I was mocking her about her sickness. She became ill with the Covid demon. While we were talking, she claimed being on her death bed. I countered the comment with a faith statement, saying, "You shall live and not die. You are not on your death bed," She took that as me saying she wasn't that sick. She didn't speak to me for two months. Once we finally spoke again, I asked why did you hang up on me and stop talking to me? She then told me how she perceived my statements, and that they made her angry. I went on to inquire of her about the faith statements and how could God's word be taken any other way? I also acknowledged the fact that they were very true. "We are talking now; you didn't die." If me speaking the word of God over you or your situation angers you then check yourself not me. I would say the same thing all over again if I had to. I would never agree to speak death over you or anyone at all ever. The fact that she went months not talking to me for such a fixable moment; let me know that our friendship is not as strong and embedded as I thought it was. This is what the bible talks about; having ought against your brother or sister, lay your gift down and go and make peace with them. Then go back and offer your gift to the Lord. I have not been the same with her since that happened.

You see how anger, rage, misunderstandings, lack of communication, and frustration all keep us in a mode of offense, defense, and simply out of the Love Walk God has demonstrated for us to possess. We must obey the word completely to obtain the gifts and standards that He has left for us to conqueror this world and everything in it.

Phil. 4:19 Always!

<u>My Thoughts and Emotions</u>

_____

_____

_____

_____

_____

    I became one of the leaders in the Awakening the Diamonds sisterhood. In one of my meetings we talked about finding our identity in God. We also discussed the calls of God over our lives and how we responded to the calls. Previously in this unit, we've identified some of our under-currents, how would you respond to the call on your life?

_____

_____

_____

_____

_____

    Are you aware that you deal with rejection or anger issues?

_____

_____

_____

_____

_____

6. When did you recognize that your anger was an issue?

_____

_____

_____

_____

7. How do you feel about the rejection or anger that you feel?

_____

_____

_____

_____

8. Do you try to curve your anger? What do you do to reverse your actions when angry or feeling rejected?

_____

_____

_____

_____

9. How does your anger or rejection affect certain areas of your life?

_____

_____

_____

_____

10. If you could release the anger, smothered hostility, fear of rejection, and other insecurities caused by the spirit of rejection; Would you work at achieving total deliverance? Would you be willing to submit totally to the Holy Spirit and trust God to heal those hidden areas? (The spirit of rejection is birth through a lot of other open spiritual portals that are only shut through total deliverance.)

_____

_____

_____

_____

WALKING OUT THE PROCESS !

I'm a Butterfly!!

Unit II, Part 1
Hanging in the Cocoon

In the name of Jesus Christ, Lord we ask that you come into our hearts now and remove all discouragement, and disappointment. Lord give us the strength to see the day as yours and we shall rejoice and be glad in it. Lord let us remember that your joy is our strength, and all of our help comes from you. Father, keep us in your divine light and continuously direct our path. Lord remind us daily that you are with us and we're never alone. Keep us in perfect peace and renew our minds. In Jesus name Amen.

DEPRESSION

Depression has been known to paralyze many of us, keep us in bondage, binding us to isolation, and in some cases, drinking, drugs, sex addiction, and other dysfunctional behaviors. We push away the very people that want to help us and invite in those we should push away. Depression is a spirit and it's demonic. God is not connected to depression or it's symptoms in anyway. We know that it's a known medical condition; those of us walking in the spirit know that we use doctors and trust God. Some cases actually need medication to help their situation; by no means am I saying not to seek professional medical assistance if you can't pray your way out the violating clutch of depression.

I know all too well of the dark hole mentally and emotionally that it can push you into. If it wasn't for my prayer life and faith in God; I don't know how I would have made it through those times. Depression has pushed people to commit suicide, murder, self-mutilation, and other degrading acts. Why? Most of the people that allow the enemy to control their thoughts sometimes are not connected to God whole heartedly and then there are those who love God with all their heart; but still can't seem to fight off this intruding demon. When we seek God whole heartedly, it keeps us grounded and he continuously renews our minds. The Holy Spirit gives us strength to bare the attacks of the enemy. When we have the Holy Spirit inside of us; it leads us, guides us, warns us, informs us, and it will always protect us. The bible says that God always gives us a way of escape from every situation. We have to take the escape; sometimes we don't listen to the still voice inside that says don't do a certain thing, don't go a certain place, don't say something, and don't deal with a particular person. Instead, we move on in our fleshly decisions, listening to the carnal mind.

*{The World Organization says: Sep 13, 2021 — Depression is a common illness worldwide, an **estimated 3.8% of the population are affected**, including 5.0% among adults and 5.7% among adults older than 60 years old}*

<u>My Thoughts and Emotions</u>

_____

_____

_____

_____

11. Are you aware of what depression looks and feels like?

_____

_____

_____

_____

12. Have you ever experienced depression? If so, what did it feel like?

_____

_____

_____

_____

_____

_____

13. How did you deal with most days? Where did you pull your strength from?

_____

_____

_____

_____

_____

_____

14. What do you think you would do different, right now, if depression tried to return?

_____

_____

_____

_____

_____

15. For those of you that maybe still struggling with this debilitating sickness, paralyzing demon. How would you feel about trying new techniques to deal with depression? Are you willing to trust God wholeheartedly with your situation?

_____

_____

_____

_____

_____

Unit II, Part 2
Hanging in the Cocoon

Lord help us see today as the day you've made and help us rejoice and be glad in it. God help us see the joy of the Lord as being our strength. Father God, we need you to teach us, save us, and set us free from all the plots of the devil. Lord, we know that we are never alone, because you are always with us. Lord renew our minds and help us pull down every thought that tries to exalt itself over the things of God. In Jesus name, we yield our bodies over to you and ask that you pour into us all the fruits of the spirit. In Jesus name, Lord help us to see, feel, and hear you clearly. We break the bondage and torment of the spirit of loneliness and ask that you fill us up with your love and encouragement in Jesus name Amen !!

Loneliness

Loneliness has caused some to take their own life; and others enter relationships that they know are not for them. It will cause you to settle with an unequally yoked person as a life partner. The spirit of abandonment will constantly make you feel rejected and alone. We continuously look in the wrong places for love and acceptance. The spirit of loneliness have caused a lot of people of God to move ahead of the Lord and give up on His promises and take things into their own hands and make little Ishmaels all over the place. I know all too well about battling the spirit of loneliness. I did all the above trying to find love and companionship in all the wrong places.

Not recognizing my own self-worth. I allowed the enemy to play with my mind and found myself in bad relationships with people I should have never been *entangled* with; allowing them to draw me into soul ties that I should have seen far in advance. The spirit of loneliness is blinding to the things of God if you are not praying and walking in discernment. Despair and discouragement takes over your thoughts. We have to go through serious sincere deliverance.

The spirit of rejection will give birth to the spirit of abandonment and loneliness and will become a stronghold if not addressed and dealt with. If we do not renew our minds with the word of God and sincerely see things for what they really are and call them out. We will find ourselves compromising, settling, and committing to false obligations wherever we feel needed or accepted.

<u>My Thoughts and Emotions</u>

_____

_____

_____

_____

_____

16. If and whenever you feel lonely; what do you do? Who do you call?

_____

_____

_____

_____

_____

17. When abandonment tries to attack you; do you recognize it? Do you resist it or give into the emotions of this spirit?

_____

_____

_____

_____

_____

18. If you had a way of escape every time your emotions flared up in your mind and heart; would you take it? (God always gives us a way of escape from issues or temptations)

_____

_____

_____

_____

_____

19. Do you know the first time you felt lonely, abandoned, worthless? Do you know who made you feel these emotions?

_____

_____

_____

_____

_____

_____

20. How do you deal with these emotions now as an adult? What steps do you take to protect yourself from this debilitating sickness and or spirits?

_____

_____

_____

_____

_____

Hanging in the Cocoon !!

I'm a Butterfly!!

Unit III
Breakthrough To Greatness

Lord Jesus, touch every soul that reads this book and strengthen them Father God in every area of their lives. Lord this unit is incredibly special to my heart. God, the spirit of perversion and entrapment was so strong in my life; I pray this day and daily that no person be trapped in their minds and body to that magnitude! In Jesus name! I pray for your children to be free. I pray that your parents and loved ones, and or you be set free from the bondages of perversion and the generational curses of rejection that may lead to perversion. Lord in the name of Jesus, we come against this spirit with the blood of Jesus and cast it back to outer darkness from which it comes. God, I pray that anyone reading this book be free in Jesus name!! Lord, I speak total healing and deliverance FROM MOLESTATION, PORNOGRAPHY, LESBIANISM, HOMOSEXUALITY, CROSS DRESSING, GENDER CONFUSION, PEDOPHILIA, PROSTITUTION, SEX TRAFFICING, PIMPING, and all others, Satan release the minds of these people, In Jesus's name let them go. Lord help them understand this is not behavior of you. We walk in total health and healing. God send full deliverance and redemption for those that want your salvation. Lord, I thank you and I praise you that lives will be changed forever for Your Glory and the building of the kingdom. Amen!!

<u>Sexual Temptation and Traps</u>

Well, this is the most controversial unit in this book. I didn't place it here to argue or debate. I am here to help those who seek a way out and feel stuck in certain situations. I am here to offer practical biblical solutions to some major world problems if people would only listen and trust God fully with their lives and issues.

Coming from a life of lesbianism and bisexual practices for over 18 years; carrying over 200+ hours in counseling and social works college hours, over 20 years in deliverance ministry and 15 of those years are in leadership and evangelism; I'm here to say I am thankful that I got my identity back. The devil tried to steal my identity from me and change me from who God created me to be, to who he wanted me to be, and who society said I would be. From a straight 'A' student to a high school dropout, from a beautiful young girl with so much potential to an exotic dancer and teenage prostitute. From a girl with dreams and hopes to a girl with low self-esteem, lack of worth, and a broken spirit. From a beautiful young lady with so many gifts and talents and a lot of love to give; one that any man would want to have her as a wife, to a woman that trusted no one and lowered her standards to except the lowest of lovers and mates to avoid being alone.

God himself gave his only son for my life. For me to be forgiven for my sins. A brain to think on these things: whatever is true, whatever is noble, whatever is right, whatever is pure, whatever is lovely, whatever is admirable—if anything is excellent or praiseworthy—think about such things. **<u>{Philippians 4:8}</u>**

I can give testimony after testimony on how God has helped me and my children in our lives and may never convince you that the life you are living is not of Gods choosing for you.

I know without a doubt, because I am fearfully and wonderfully made; Your {GOD'S} works are wonderful {Psalms 139:14} I have to believe that I'm made in His imagine. God created mankind in his own image, in the image of God he created them; male and female he created them. {Genesis 1:27} If all that be true then how can the image of pornography, homosexuality, cross dressing, gender confusion, prostitution, sexual immortality, exhibitionist behavior, adulterous, fornicator, and whoremonger, be my image too?

Understand, what I've done is not who I am, it's who the enemy wanted me to be. I am who God says I am! When I accepted Christ into my life, I started to act more like Him, talk about Him, think like Him. My true image started to show through the cocoon. The butterfly started to form and turn around in that small space of sin and dirt. The transformation started to take place. The life of that woman was no longer dark and headed downward. Many beautiful colors started to form, change began, and it felt good. Fruits of the spirit started to take demand over her character flaws. She started to feel smart, pretty, important, and loved again. There's a spot in a cocoon for you to make your transformation as well. God wants to give you your true identity. Not the tag or title that the enemy gave you in the world. Throw those grave clothes away and allow the Lord to redress you properly for where He wants to take you. We can be totally free and redeemed. We can live a life of liberty.

The devil wants us in shame, despair, hidden, and sneaking in dark places like roaches in a dark room. Jesus died so that we would have life and have it more abundantly. God wishes that we prosper and be in good health as our soul prospers {3John 1:2}. We don't have to sleep around to get our needs met; God will meet all your needs according to the riches of His Glory in Christ Jesus {Phil. 4:19}. We don't need to have some person making business deals over our bodies. We can present our bodies as living sacrifices Holy and acceptable unto God which is our reasonable service. {Romans 12:1}

Please make a mental note that all prostitutes don't walk the streets or work for a pimp or call service. They are regular women living regular everyday lives. She's the one that takes that call from the guy that pays her rent or light bill and he only does after they have sex and tries to control her even though he's not committed to her. She's that woman that calls that special friend over only when she's in need of money and knows all the right things to say and do to him to get whatever she wants from him; They fall in with sugar babies. Those sugar daddies are not your source! God should be your source and Him alone. But sometimes we forget all that our God owns All the cattle on a thousand hills, and we don't have to depend on or be mistreated by anyone for anything we need. We only have to believe and follow our Savior's plan for our lives. We'll talk more about that in the next unit.

Sex trafficking, pimping, exhibitionist behavior, pedophilia, child pornography, molestation and other violations are all illegal activities. Therefore, we surely without doubt know those are not of God. Yet, we still find Christians and non-believers caught up these various acts. Now, we obviously see that God created the order of mankind by making a man and woman. SO, we know without any doubt that same sex relationships and practices are surely not a signature of God's work. HE DID NOT START THE WORLD THAT WAY. It was never meant for us, but the enemy said aww, come on you don't have to just settle for her; you can have him and her and the child too. Do them all and the animals too if you want to. All of that was a trick from the enemy to have people deceived and lost to who God really wants us to be. I'm a living testimony that God wants us whole, healed, redeemed, and set free. Jesus wants our minds renewed and our hearts free of all disappointments and discouragement.

I'm here to give some biblical practical principles to help guide you to transformation. Only if this is what you want for yourself, it's a free decision that you make. Liberty and deliverance or bondage and despair. This is where you decide what's more important to you at this point. Your love life and flesh or your soul when you die. Quick gratification here on earth or everlasting life in heaven with our Lord and Savior Jesus Christ?

If serving the LORD seems undesirable to you, then choose for yourselves this day whom you will serve, whether the gods your ancestors served beyond the Euphrates, or the gods of the Amorites, in whose land you are living. But as for me and my household, we will serve the LORD." {Joshua 24: 15}

<u>My Thoughts and Emotions</u>

_____

_____

_____

_____

_____

21. How did you come to the decision that you wanted to live your life in gender confusion? (Woman acting and pretending to be a man & a man taking on the full characteristics of a woman {sex changes})

_____

_____

_____

_____

_____

22. Why do you think that you have homosexual or lesbian tendencies?

_____

_____

_____

_____

_____

23. Did something traumatic happen to you? Did this event cause you to feel like you could never be with the opposite sex?

_____

_____

_____

_____

24. Who told you that selling your body for money was an effective way to make money? (Someone offered it to me as learning the business, I could make me a lot of money as a madame. He told me as his woman I would be in charge of all the girls and first I had to learn the business. That story is discussed in another book☺)

_____

_____

_____

_____

25. Where did you get the idea that showing off your body parts for arousal to innocent bystanders or for payment was okay to do?

_____

_____

_____

_____

_____

26. What person loves you enough? Would God say it is okay? Where do you think the thought came from one day in someone's head? To say it was okay for a man or woman to take young girls or boys and teach them how to prostitute their bodies and they benefit from the work the kids do? {I really want you to concentrate on this question if this was your experience. Because I really want you to see how the enemy tried to trick you and me; tried to kill us before we could figure out who we really are to God}

_____

_____

_____

_____

The sex traps and scandals in this country alone are huge and phenomenally growing bigger every day according to statistics and society.

{National arrest figures [in the United States] range over 100,000. The National Task Force on Prostitution suggests that **over one million people in the US have worked as prostitutes in the United States**, or about 1% of American women." Jan 11, 2018}

With that being said, the traps that are set for our spouses, children and ourselves are overwhelming. It's *almost* impossible not to become victim or entangled in some type of sex scandal when it's everywhere; all around you all the time.

Perversion is being poured out on our children excessively. We are teaching them one way at home; they go to school or turn on the television and there's same sex couples everywhere cheering on homosexuality and lesbianism and or bi- sexual behavior. We are trying to protect our families to best of our ability in every area. But, the prince of the air, the enemy is working overtime to confuse the minds of our children and make them believe that they don't have to be with a boy or a girl. Society is influenced by the things of the devil to say our kids have the right to decide as a "child" to be something other than what they were born as. I was one of those children and it wasn't all over the TV and in my school. But there were older perverted men and women that introduced me to all these new ways of doing things.

If husbands would only enjoy their own wives and wives only enjoy their own husbands, then the adultery rate would drop. You're married but you're not satisfied with the spouse you chose?! The acts of fornication was lowered dramatically after HIV/ Aides hit the USA, but it soon returned to an all-time high as does all other sins. People no longer want to be with just their spouses, but now want to bring in 1 or 2 others into the bedroom to "spice it up". Back in the day this was called swingers, threesomes', and orgies (group sex). All of this is a trick of the devil. Every one of these are traps to keep people from being faithful to God, their spouses, and from making a commitment to someone that could possibly become your spouse. It offers a fake sense of security and instant gratification, which will lead nowhere but sin and death.

It is statistically proven that these traps and snares are sweeping across the country. The sex traffic scam is huge. Most women have stopped going out working for another person. They become 'independent contractors' or liberated sex workers; (a woman or man paid {in monetary or goods} for sexual encounters of All sorts) willing to be paid for the things that your spouse won't do at home).

They steal young girls because the supply of workers is low, and they want to keep making money, same as the slave trade. Young children and woman are most often forced into this life by drug addiction and severe abuse. It's imperative that we take care of our young women and protect them at all costs. Educate them on what's going on and how it can subtly be introduced to them and the lures of these traps.

<u>My Thoughts and Emotions</u>

_____

_____

_____

_____

_____

_____

27. The traps that you may have been caught in, in the past or now; have they left any good thing in your life?

_____

_____

_____

_____

_____

28. If you chose a certain person to spend the rest of your life; why do you cheat on them? Who told you that behavior was acceptable?

_____

_____

_____

_____

_____

29. Why do you settle for being someone's side chick or dude? Are you not good enough for someone special or to be #1 to someone?

_____

_____

_____

_____

30. Have you thought about how different it would be if you did everything [as much as possible] the way that God said to do it? What would life be like for you and your family?

_____

_____

_____

_____

31. Think back to when you were first hurt, touched, or introduce to sexual immortality. When did you first think that you would need a "sugar daddy", or that your body was so pretty that you would sell it to make money? That person that lured you into that life did not love you and the devil wanted you dead before you could find out who you really were in God.

_____

_____

_____

_____

Breakthrough to Greatness !!

I'm a Butterfly!!

Unit IV Part 1
Spread your Wings

Jesus continue to move through our lives in every area of our lives. Lord here we are, we have back tracked through some hurting times. We have had to remember painful events and moments. Lord send peace and contentment as we go through our full deliverance in what issues/sin that you have found in our hearts and lives. In Jesus Name, please Lord move out everything that is unlike you, God. Lord search our hearts to the deepest parts and replace all the foul ground with your love, peace, joy, contentment, encouragement, honesty, and patience. Lord, we have brought all of our issues and problems to you and laid them out on the alter at the feet of Jesus. Help us today Lord to move forward in our full deliverance. God, we know it will take more than reading this book and bible. Jesus, we need a regular intake of your word and anointing from the Holy Spirit with keeping power. Lord save us, redeem us, deliver us, teach us, show us, and draw us closer to your ways and principles. Lord make us and mold us to be more like your son Jesus!! We surrender it all to you Lord. We release all unforgiveness and anger, rage, perversion, sexual immortality, control, abuse, lying, bad attitudes and tempers to you God. Knowing that you are faithful to forgive us and renew us. All in Jesus name Amen, Amen !!!

Deliverance

If you have made it to this unit and are still willing to give God the reigns to your life this is a wonderful time to shout HALLELUJAH!!!! You have made one of the biggest steps of your life. To come to or rededicate your life to Jesus Christ is one of the most valuable investments you could ever make in yourself.

Because the perks that come with salvation and deliverances are irreplaceable, undeniable, and no job could ever offer you a package like this one.

Deliverance, liberation, freedom, rescued, saved, loosed; all these words are exciting when thinking about your life, mind, and heart. We must go through the deliverance process with all sincerity; knowing that God knows what's best for our life. Repentance- means to regret or being remorsefully sorry for the things we've done or didn't do that we should've done. Lord, we are sorry for all of our sins and truly DO NOT want to keep doing them. Lord, we humble ourselves at your feet and ask that you come into our hearts and make us clean and new. {Romans 10:9} Help us learn your ways and understand our purpose. Lead and guide us by your Holy Spirit to the place where we can grow in your word. Mature, be free, delivered leaders solely and concerned about building the saints for the work of the kingdom. So, now we take our deliverance profoundly serious same as an addict or alcoholic takes their sobriety serious. We work at staying delivered from our shortcomings and we make deliberate decisions to walk a path of righteousness and faith.

My Thoughts and Emotions

I'm a Butterfly!!

32. Do you understand what deliverance really is? Do you think that you have experienced it?

_____

_____

_____

_____

_____

33. Do you know how to maintain your deliverance? Are you willing to give up certain things and people in order to demand your peace in your time of deliverance?

_____

_____

_____

_____

_____

34. Have you had a pastor, spiritual teacher, (Holy Ghost filled), bishop, or evangelist help you to discover or walk you through your deliverance process?

_____

_____

_____

_____

_____

35. Do you believe that you were delivered the moment you asked God for deliverance?

_____

_____

_____

_____

_____

I'm a Butterfly!!

Unit IV Part 2
Spread your Wings

Lord it is our obedience to your words and your commands that touch you. Faith without works is dead. We have faith that you have forgiven us and renewed our minds. Now, Lord we want to be busy working out our salvation with fear and trembling. Obeying you in every way we humanly can. God, we want to please you with our actions, talk, walk, thoughts, deeds, and attitudes. Jesus left an example on how we should live and carry ourselves on earth. Lord, we want to follow that example as much as we possibly can. Lord not being spooky and self-righteous; but faith walkers and obeying your word to the fullest. In Jesus Name. Amen!!

Obedience

Well, here we are, we have survived the cocoon, we made it through transformation. We walked through the process, and we have received our deliverance. Now it is time for us to walk in obedience. Which is easier said than done. To obey God's word and commands is to deny yourself of your personal will or thoughts. To obey God is a mega tool used in our restoration and transformation. The main component missing today in our Christian experience is OBEDIENCE, which is a Valuable Core element and the true test of our faith. We quote "faith without works is dead" all the time; But Faith is an act of obedience. We have to believe, if we obey God's instructions that it will produce that thing, we are believing God for. Do you see the correlation?

Ok, look, the scriptures say, "without faith it's impossible to please God" Well, to obey God means we must have the faith that God is who He is. Then we believe that God can do what He says

He will do. Finally, we move on the instructions He gives us to obtain a certain thing. There it is, we've moved toward obedience and God will move on our behalf. Obedience is so particularly important to God that He said in His word that "obedience is better than sacrifice"

God wants us to move when He says, do when He says to do, and go where He tells us to go. I personally know people that have received instructions from God and flat out did not obey. They did not give what God told them too, they didn't buy what they were supposed to buy, they didn't sow into the person God told them too. All of this is disobedience and are clear scenarios of lack of Faith. The Lord personally trained me to hear His voice in multiple actions. He would give me specific assignments and I would carry them out. For example, one time I was taking my friend a card and balloons to her job; because she had been working really hard and was being mistreated by a few co-workers. But, on the way into her workplace, which was a hospital, there was a lady sitting on a bench right as you walk into the door. We greeted one another, smiled and I continued on my way to the nearest elevator. Maybe 3 feet pass her I clearly heard give her those balloons. I responded in my mind with the thought, "these balloons are for my sister". Only to hear it again and louder, "Give her those balloons". I said, "Lord, I bought these for my sister, and you want me to give them to this lady?" Again, "Give her those balloons and tell her that I love her!" I turned around, because by this time I'm about 10 feet from her; went up to her and said, "Hi, ma'am The Lord says{He loves you and wants you to have these balloons}, God bless you". The lady excepted the balloons and started seriously crying; while saying thank you to me. I turned to walk away; I got maybe 3 ft. away from her and she slightly yelled thanks again sweetie. I looked at her and smiled and looked at the door as she was getting up like her ride HAD ARRIVED. I see a cab sitting in the driveway of the doorway; she proceeded to walk to the cab; with a brace on her leg and cane. I got sad immediately; asking God, "Lord, she had no one to pick her up from the hospital"?

See, we say {something said I should do this or that} {something told me not to go there or to do this or that} If it's something good and going to help you are someone else it's the Lord speaking to your heart or the Holy Spirit trying to guide us and or protect us. NOT SOMETHING SAID. Another time, I was riding down the street listen to my music loudly, a few days after the Hurricane Katrina had pushed busloads of people to Houston, Texas in the Astro dome or NRG center. As I sat at a red light there was a lady sitting at the bus stop, I heard, "give her $10.00". Light turned green. I said," oohh, I am already across the light now. I heard louder, "turn around and go bk; give her ten dollars". So, I did. I turned my car around and went bk, pulled into the station where the bus stop was sitting. I got out and she got up looking toward my direction, looking to see if her bus was coming. I yelled to her, "excuse me ma'am. I need to give you this". Holding the ten dollar bill up for her to see it, she walked toward me, we met, and I proceeded to tell her that God wanted her to have it and be blessed. She responded with a sincere thank you and said "I'm on my way to the Astro dome to look for some family members that was bussed here and I had no clue how I was going to get them bk to my house. I did not have enough money to pay all of their bus fares. Ma'am this is truly sent from God". I said, "ma'am be careful be blessed". Went bk to my car and cried all the way down that boulevard. Thinking what if I would not have listened to the assignment. God is serious about providing our every need. The stories go on and on, that is just a couple to let you know that God does speak to us. We just have to listen, be willing, and obey. He will always execute the plan perfectly.

Our lives and maintaining our deliverance is the same way. He will direct us on where to go, when to go, who to speak to and how we should do whatever it is He wants us to do. Yes, we all want to be wealthy and live well; however, all of our lives are not destined to riches and glamour; that's the reality. Sometimes God blesses us as we go along; with good health and strong families. Great ministries and serious assignments;

are we willing to be faithful over a few things even if it doesn't bring fame and fortune? If we're not in the spotlight as the big wheel, or the biggest church or not even a popular praise and worship leader. Blessings on blessings are actually connected to our obedience. I obeyed God and paid a few folks accounts and let them get their things out of the delinquent storages whenever God told me to; in turn years later when me and my family went through challenging times and had 2 storages, we never lost our things; because of the seeds I had sown in the past when God said to do so. Our blessings are connected to various things, and we miss it by not obeying God. Visa versa, we gain them when we do obey very step that God speaks to us.

Obey God, by leaving the situation that's not good for you or edifying you in Gods will. Obey by, giving something to someone that you know it's been on your heart, but you allowed your senses to talk you out of doing the assignment. Obey God with your finances; give money to folks that have been in a tough time, and you know you have the funds to help them. Do it. Don't miss your blessings by being stubborn or selfish.

Obey God, when you clearly heard in your heart to get up and read your bible, go to church, pray more, talk to a loved one or neighbor, or anyone about salvation and redemption. All these are ways we can obey God and release our own blessings in any areas.

My Thoughts and Emotions

_____

_____

_____

_____

_____

_____

36. How much are you willing to give to be obedient to the Lord? {not money or material things even though that requires your obedience also} But to give of yourself, time, and energy, all things that you can not get back once it's gone.

_____

_____

_____

_____

_____

37. Your obedience may require some embarrassments or humbling at some point. You may be required to do things that your flesh, mind, or heart just doesn't want to do. Will you obey God in spite of how you might feel naturally?

_____

_____

_____

_____

_____

38. Can you honestly say for God I live -for God I'll die? When it's concerning your children or a loved one?

_____

_____

_____

_____

39. When God gives us assignments, they are not always things we favor; or what we'd choose to do in some circumstances. Will you fully obey the instructions of the Lord?

_____

_____

_____

_____

_____

Spread Your Wings !!

I'm a Butterfly!!

Unit V
Be Free

Father God, help us walk in our newness; while teaching us how to be free in your love and grace. Lord your word says, "there's no condemnation in us that are in Christ Jesus" Remind us of that daily. Lord help us see ourselves like you see us. Lead us into the doors you want us to enter, and slam shut tight the ones you don't want us to enter in Jesus name. Father God, we love you and thank you for your undying love towards us. Lord, we have been freed from our cocoons of shame, defeat, rejection, anger, depression, loneliness, sexual sins, and perversions, discouragement, and lack of self-worth. Thank you father G0d, for life and abundance in joy, peace, contentment, hope, love, and good health. Lord, we know following you and being renewed in your glory doesn't mean we won't have problems or issues. But we now have your peace and joy, the Holy Spirit to help us endure as a good soldier. Not giving into sin, shame, and despair. We ARE OVERCOMERS AND REDEEMED BY THE BLODD OF JESUS CHRIST !!!!!!!!!!!!!!!!! HALLELUJAH !!!!!!!!!!!!!!!!!!

AMEN, AMEN, AMEN !!!!!!!!!!!!!!!!!!!!!!!!!!!

LIBERTY

Thank you, Jesus!! If you have walked through this devotional continuously to this point, I pray you feel so much better than when you began this book. I thank you for taking the time to see about yourself. Lord, you said "whom you set free is free indeed". Our liberty means, we are free to live out the latter days of our lives without guilt, shame, regrets, and disappointments. The enemy can no longer hold us bound to our pass mistakes or setbacks. We have broken out the cocoons and have gained strong, beautiful wings to fly high and far. We are not our pass or our experiences; but we are new creatures. Reborn, redeemed, remade, rebuilt, minds renewed, all old things have passed away and nothing that looks like our past can attach itself to us.

We are not associated or attached to any old soul ties, demonic thought processes, or debilitating habits that can cause us to slip out of our new path of righteousness. We have become sons and daughters of Christ and no longer walk after the things of our flesh and thoughts of the enemy. We are created in the image of God and have no reason at all to go into caves of hiding and seclusion in darkness of our old mindsets.

I am so happy to share with you this love and peace that I received from God. Say this with me as we close our last unit. Lord, thank you for saving me. You are my Lord and savior, thank you for dying on the cross for my sins. Thank you, God, for loving me and not letting me die in the craziness I was walking for so long. Thank Father, for keeping your hand on my life and not leaving me to a reprobate mind. I believe that you have forgiven me, and I forgive myself and others. Every person that operated against me, touch me wrong, talked to me wrong, labeled me, and abandoned me. I love you Jesus and I have no need to hold on to those hurting things or people anymore. IN JESUS NAME AMEN.

I AM FREE !!!! TO BE ME !!!!!!! THE ME YOU CREATED ME TO BE!!!!!!!!

Romans 10: 9-10

{If you declare with your mouth, "Jesus is Lord," and believe in your heart that God raised him from the dead, you will be saved. 10 For it is with your heart that you believe and are justified, and it is with your mouth that you profess your faith and are saved.}

<u>My Thoughts and Emotions</u>

_____

_____

_____

_____

_____

_____

40. How do you feel?

_____

_____

_____

_____

_____

_____

41. Do you truly feel liberated? What areas do you feel free in?

_____

_____

_____

_____

_____

_____

42. Can you use this book over again ? Yes. You can get a notebook and go over any area you need to as many times as you need to; maintain your deliverance. Do you think your mind is renewed?

_____

_____

_____

_____

_____

_____

Be Free !!!

Here's some scriptures for you to meditate over.

These scriptures included will help you understand why you haven't heard God or didn't recognize His voice.

I Samuel 3: 1-21, Approximately 11 years old ~ {He didn't understand it was God calling him}

Exodus 3: 11 But Moses said to God, "Who am I, that I should go to Pharaoh and bring the Israelites out of Egypt? {We have questioned our self-worth}

Exodus 4:10 But Moses pleaded with the LORD, "O Lord, I'm not very good with words. I never have been, and I'm not now, even though you have spoken to me. I get tongue-tied, and my words get tangled. {We see everything wrong with ourselves and can't recognize our own strengths and gifts}

Exodus 6:30 But Moses argued with the LORD, saying, "I can't do it! I'm such a clumsy speaker! Why should Pharaoh listen to me?" {We constantly give God excuses, instead of being all so ready to obey Him.}

Genesis 37:5-6 (17 yrs. old) Joseph had a dream, and when he told it to his brothers, they hated him all the more. He said to them, "Listen to this dream I had" {some of us heard God's voice and knew it was the Lord. Rebellion, fear, and intimidation come in and distracted us from our divine destiny and purpose. We shared the news or instruction w/ others that are not happy about our coat of colors.}

Let's go ahead and begin peeling back the layers of this Cocoon.

Unit 1 Rejection

Psalm 34:18 *Isaiah 41:10* *Proverbs 3:5-6*
Psalm 73:26 *Revelation 21:4* *Psalm 147:3*
1 Corinthians 13:7 *2 Corinthians 5:7* *John 14:27*
Psalm 55:22 *Matthew 11:28-30* *Philippians 4:13*
2 Corinthians 12:9 *John 14:13*

Unit 1 Anger

Psalms 5: 11-12 *Jeremiah 30:17* *Isaiah 62:3-4*
 Romans 8:15-16
James 1:19-20 *Proverbs 29:11* *Ephesians 4:26-31*
 Proverbs 19:11

Unit 2 Depression

Psalm 9:9 Psalm 30:5 Psalm 34:17-18
Isaiah 41:10 Proverbs 3:5-6 Philippians 4:6-7
Revelation 21:4 Philippians 4:13 Joshua 1:9

Unit 2 Loneliness

2 Corinthians 4:17 Psalm 17:15 Colossians 3:1-4
 Psalm 139:7-10 Isaiah 58:11
Philippians 4:19 Joshua 1:5-6 Isaiah 41:10

Unit 3 Sexual Temptation

Joshua 24:15 3 John 1:2 Phil 4:8,19
Romans 12:1 Romans 6:1 Galatians 5:22-23
Isaiah 26:3 Ezekiel 33:9 Ezekiel 3:18
 Genesis 1:27

Unit 4 Deliverance

2 Timothy 4:18	2 Timothy 3:11	2 Peter 2:9
2 Corinthians 1:10	1 Thessalonians 1:10	

Unit 4 Obedience

1 Samuel 15:22	James 1:22	Isaiah 1:19
Luke 6:46	John 14:15	James 4:7
John 14:21	Exodus 19:5	1 Peter 1:14

Unit V Liberty

2 Corinthians 3:17	John 8:32	1 Peter 2:16-17
Galatians 5:1	Romans 13:8	Galatians 5:13
Psalm 118:5	John 8:36	Romans 8:2

Isaiah 61:1

"The Spirit of the Lord God is upon me, Because the Lord has anointed me to bring good news to the afflicted; He has sent me to bind up the brokenhearted, to proclaim liberty to captives and freedom to prisoners."

From the Author:

I pray that this book has been a great help to you. It was helping me while I was writing it. I love you wherever you are in the world reading this and writing out your responses. Be free to be you. Your unapologetic God made self. I thank God for His undying love towards us. I pray that you share this book with someone that you may know who needs to be free too. Take care of yourself and I am excited to know that we'll be celebrating in Heaven together someday. Stay free!!

Blessings and Grace,

Evangelist Toshia

<u>*I AM A BUTTERFLY !!*</u>

<u>NOTES</u>

_____

_____

_____

_____

_____

_____

_____

_____

_____

_____

_____

_____

_____

_____

_____

_____

_____

_____

I'm a Butterfly!!

<u>NOTES</u>

_____

_____

_____

_____

_____

_____

_____

_____

_____

_____

_____

_____

_____

_____

_____

_____

_____

_____

_____

I'm a Butterfly!!

<u>NOTES</u>

_____

_____

_____

_____

_____

_____

_____

_____

_____

_____

_____

_____

_____

_____

_____

_____

_____

Printed in the United States
by Baker & Taylor Publisher Services